WINTER
TREE FINDER

Identifying Deciduous Trees in Winter

MAY THEILGAARD WATTS and TOM WATTS

**Nature Study
Guild Publishers**
an imprint of AdventureKEEN

HOW TO USE THIS BOOK

1. Select a typical twig of the tree you wish to identify. Avoid freaks. (If you cut the twig, do it straight across and sharply to prevent distortion of the pith and damage to the tree.)

2. Begin on page 6 and proceed step by step, considering each choice. (There is a scale for measuring on the cover.)

3. When you have made the final choice, arriving at the name of the tree, compare your twig with the illustration, and check other features shown.

Advice: Examine pages 1 to 5 before starting on page 6.

This book is for deciduous trees in winter. For evergreens, or when trees have leaves, use *Tree Finder*.

Area covered by this book

A good number of the trees in this book are introduced or naturalized species. Some, such as tree of heaven (page 9), are now considered *invasive* and have a negative impact on the environment. To learn more about invasive trees near you, check with your state department of natural resources or environmental management agency or visit: www.invasivespeciesinfo.gov

© 2024 Keen Communications; © 1970 Nature Study Guild • ISBN 978-0-912550-45-9 • Printed in China • Cataloging-in-Publication data is available from the Library of Congress • naturestudy.com

THE PARTS OF A TWIG (Twig illustrations in this book are about ⅔ life-size.)

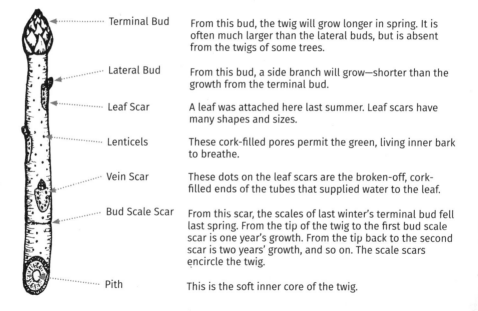

Terminal Bud

From this bud, the twig will grow longer in spring. It is often much larger than the lateral buds, but is absent from the twigs of some trees.

Lateral Bud

From this bud, a side branch will grow—shorter than the growth from the terminal bud.

Leaf Scar

A leaf was attached here last summer. Leaf scars have many shapes and sizes.

Lenticels

These cork-filled pores permit the green, living inner bark to breathe.

Vein Scar

These dots on the leaf scars are the broken-off, cork-filled ends of the tubes that supplied water to the leaf.

Bud Scale Scar

From this scar, the scales of last winter's terminal bud fell last spring. From the tip of the twig to the first bud scale scar is one year's growth. From the tip back to the second scar is two years' growth, and so on. The scale scars encircle the twig.

Pith

This is the soft inner core of the twig.

2   The map next to each twig illustration shows the area where that tree grows naturally. The kinds of places within that area where the tree is likely to grow—the habitat—is shown by one of the following symbols:

SAMPLE

Streambanks, Lakeshores ⎤
                        ⎟ Trees of these habitats often grow
Lowlands ⎦   fast and make long twigs.

Tall Forest Trees ——— These are often narrow-crowned trees without lower branches.

Under Taller Trees ——— These trees are often horizontally branched.

High Altitudes ⎤
              ⎟ These trees are also abundant in
Bogs ⎦   lowland forests of the far north.

Sand and Gravel Soil ⎤
                     ⎟ These tend to grow slowly and
Upland ⎦   make short twigs.

Edge of the Forest ——— These are often small and thorny trees.

Pioneer in Disturbed Areas ——— In time, these may hide a parking lot—or even a billboard.

THE PLACE WHERE SOME TREES GROW DEPENDS ON WHAT PEOPLE HAVE DONE, AS SHOWN BY THE FOLLOWING SYMBOLS:

Trees are planted in parks, yards, and around houses

. . . where winters are cold,

. . . where winters are mild.

Some trees came from across the sea.

Some tolerate the conditions of cities.

Pioneer trees begin to grow in a place after

soil has been disturbed,

fire,

cattle have grazed,

logging.

SOMETIMES, A CONSPICUOUS FEATURE OR THE LOCATION OF A TREE MAKES IDENTIFICATION EASIER.

Smooth, conspicuous thorns?
Try: Honey Locust
     Hawthorns

Pods?
Try: Legumes (p. 34)

Cones?
Try: Alder
     Birch Larch

Hanging balls?
Try: Sycamore
     Sweetgum

Dangling catkins?
Try: Alder
     Birch
     Ironwood

Slender trees with white or gray bark?
Try: Birch
     Aspen

Baltimore oriole's nest? Try: Elm

Acorns?
Try: Oaks

Tangled twigs (witches' brooms)?
Try: Hackberry

Empty nut husks under the tree?
Try: Hickory
     Buckeye
     Horse Chestnut

Yellow-bellied Sapsucker holes?
Try: Sugar Maple
     Mountain-Ash
     Linden

Highway planting?
Try: Pin Oak

Patches of rubbed-off–
looking bark on trunk?
Try: White Oak

Moving, boggy,
unstable, shaky
ground?
Try: Tamarack
Poison Sumac

In a fence row thicket?
Try: Hawthorns
Plum
Sumac
Cherry
Osage Orange

Does the tree reach out over a:
fisherman,
muskrat,
rowboat,
canoe?
Try: Willow

After: strip mining, bulldozers,
Army engineers,
urban renewal?

Try: Cottonwood
Box Elder

Smooth bark on trunk?
Try: Birch
Beech
Aspen

In a subdivision?
Try: Thornless Honey Locust
Pin Oak
Magnolia
Birch
Siberian Elm

Polluted urban air?
Try: Tree of Heaven
Mulberry
Sycamore
Willow

BEGIN HERE →

If the tree is a conifer and needle-bearing, but sheds its needles in the winter, go to this symbol 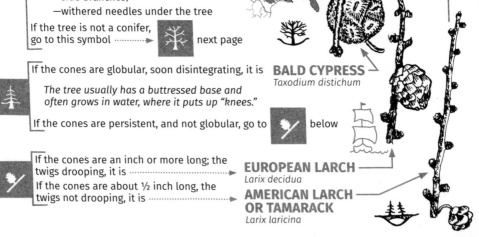 below

Conifers will have some or all of these:
—cones
—evergreen shape (central trunk all the way to the top, and small side branches)
—withered needles under the tree

If the tree is not a conifer, go to this symbol ·········→ next page

If the cones are globular, soon disintegrating, it is **BALD CYPRESS**
Taxodium distichum

The tree usually has a buttressed base and often grows in water, where it puts up "knees."

If the cones are persistent, and not globular, go to below

If the cones are an inch or more long; the twigs drooping, it is ·········→ **EUROPEAN LARCH**
Larix decidua

If the cones are about ½ inch long, the twigs not drooping, it is ·········→ **AMERICAN LARCH OR TAMARACK**
Larix laricina

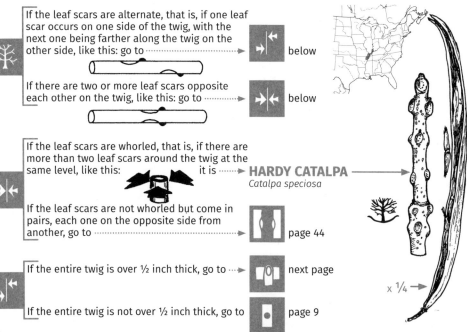

If the leaf scars are alternate, that is, if one leaf scar occurs on one side of the twig, with the next one being farther along the twig on the other side, like this: go to ⟶ below

If there are two or more leaf scars opposite each other on the twig, like this: go to ⟶ below

If the leaf scars are whorled, that is, if there are more than two leaf scars around the twig at the same level, like this: it is ⟶ **HARDY CATALPA** *Catalpa speciosa*

If the leaf scars are not whorled but come in pairs, each one on the opposite side from another, go to ⟶ page 44

If the entire twig is over ½ inch thick, go to ⟶ next page

If the entire twig is not over ½ inch thick, go to ⟶ page 9

x ¼ ⟶

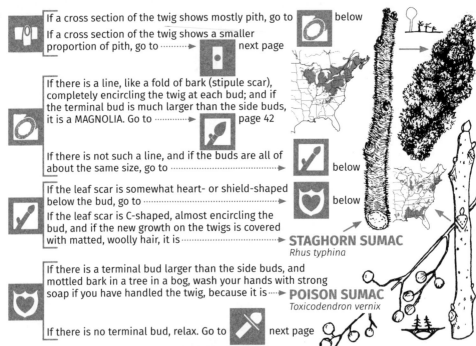

If a cross section of the twig shows mostly pith, go to below

If a cross section of the twig shows a smaller proportion of pith, go to ··········► next page

If there is a line, like a fold of bark (stipule scar), completely encircling the twig at each bud; and if the terminal bud is much larger than the side buds, it is a MAGNOLIA. Go to ··········► page 42

If there is not such a line, and if the buds are all of about the same size, go to ··········► below

If the leaf scar is somewhat heart- or shield-shaped below the bud, go to ··········► below

If the leaf scar is C-shaped, almost encircling the bud, and if the new growth on the twigs is covered with matted, woolly hair, it is ··········► **STAGHORN SUMAC**
Rhus typhina

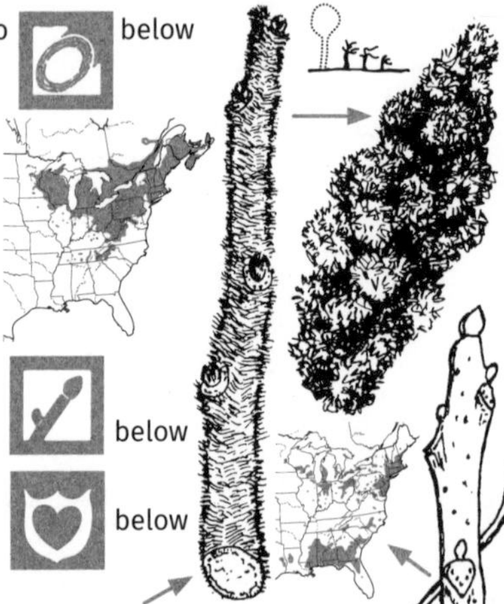

If there is a terminal bud larger than the side buds, and mottled bark in a tree in a bog, wash your hands with strong soap if you have handled the twig, because it is ····► **POISON SUMAC**
Toxicodendron vernix

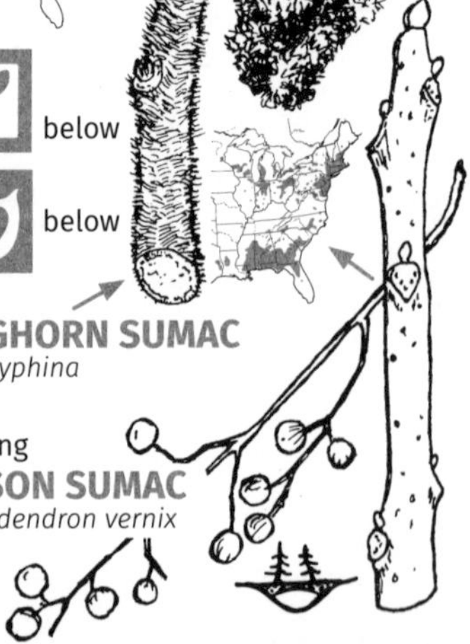

If there is no terminal bud, relax. Go to next page

If the leaf scars are marked with three to five vein scars; and two buds, depressed, looking like craters on the moon, pushed out above the leaf scar; and if the pith is thick and salmon-colored, it is ·····➤ **KENTUCKY COFFEETREE**

Gymnocladus dioicus

Mature bark has sharp, curved ridges.

If the leaf scars are marked with many vein scars, like dots, it is ···············➤ **TREE OF HEAVEN**

Ailanthus altissima

In early winter, look for the heavy clusters of winged seeds. This tree usually grows in the soot and grime of cities. The bark is smooth, with pale stripes.

If the twig is stout and tough, difficult to break, with light-colored lenticels and tan or brown pith; the leaf scars are large, pale, and somewhat heart- or shield-shaped; and the end bud is larger than the side buds, go to ··➤ page 36

If the twig does not have this combination of characteristics, go to ·················➤ next page

If several buds of different sizes are clustered irregularly at the tip of the twig, like this: 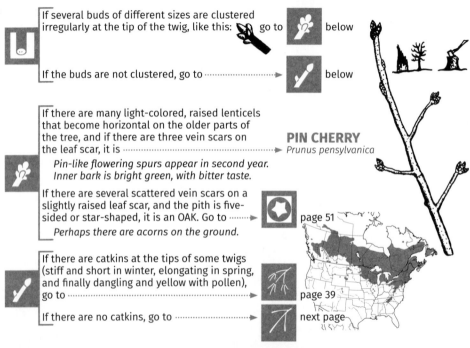 go to below

If the buds are not clustered, go to ········· ▶ below

If there are many light-colored, raised lenticels that become horizontal on the older parts of the tree, and if there are three vein scars on the leaf scar, it is ·································· ▶ **PIN CHERRY** *Prunus pensylvanica*

Pin-like flowering spurs appear in second year. Inner bark is bright green, with bitter taste.

If there are several scattered vein scars on a slightly raised leaf scar, and the pith is five-sided or star-shaped, it is an OAK. Go to ······· ▶ page 51

Perhaps there are acorns on the ground.

If there are catkins at the tips of some twigs (stiff and short in winter, elongating in spring, and finally dangling and yellow with pollen), go to ···························· ▶ page 39

If there are no catkins, go to ··············· ▶ next page

If there are protuberances on the twig (either thorns, thorn-like twigs, or rounded, stubby spurs) go to ·········· 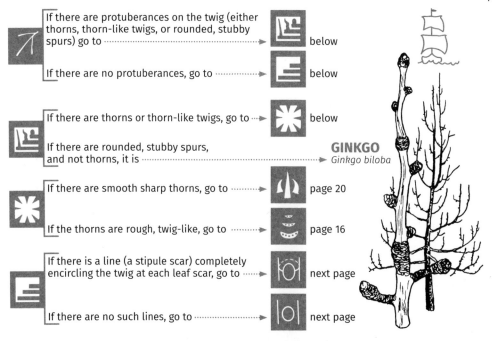 below

If there are no protuberances, go to ·········· below

If there are thorns or thorn-like twigs, go to ···· below

If there are rounded, stubby spurs, and not thorns, it is ·········· **GINKGO**
Ginkgo biloba

If there are smooth sharp thorns, go to ·········· page 20

If the thorns are rough, twig-like, go to ·········· page 16

If there is a line (a stipule scar) completely encircling the twig at each leaf scar, go to ·········· next page

If there are no such lines, go to ·········· next page

If each leaf scar completely encircles a bud; and the buds are brown, conical, with only one scale, it is ┈┈┈┈┈┈► **SYCAMORE**
Platanus occidentalis

The smooth white inner bark has flecks and patches of older bark adhering to it. The big branches look whitewashed. Look for seed balls still hanging from their long stems.

If the leaf scar does not encircle the bud, go to ┈┈┈┈► below

If the end bud is shaped like a duck bill, it is ┈┈┈► **TULIPTREE**
Liriodendron tulipifera

The main trunk usually rises straight from base to treetop.

If the end bud is not flattened like a duck bill, but is large, egg-shaped, arrowhead-shaped, or oblong, it is MAGNOLIA. Go to ┈┈┈┈► page 42

If the end of the twig is blunt, slanted, and budless (with neither terminal bud nor lateral bud); or if there are pods on the tree, it belongs to the Legume family. Go to ┈┈► page 34

If the tip of the twig does not appear blunt or budless (though there may be no true terminal bud, a lateral bud is almost in that position), go to ┈┈┈┈┈► next page

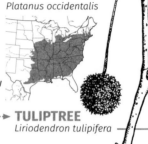

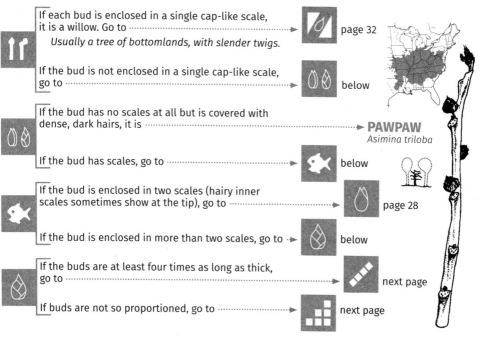

If each bud is enclosed in a single cap-like scale, it is a willow. Go to ················· → page 32

Usually a tree of bottomlands, with slender twigs.

If the bud is not enclosed in a single cap-like scale, go to ················· → below

If the bud has no scales at all but is covered with dense, dark hairs, it is ················· → **PAWPAW** *Asimina triloba*

If the bud has scales, go to ················· → below

If the bud is enclosed in two scales (hairy inner scales sometimes show at the tip), go to ················· → page 28

If the bud is enclosed in more than two scales, go to ··· → below

If the buds are at least four times as long as thick, go to ················· → next page

If buds are not so proportioned, go to ················· → next page

If the end bud is larger than the side buds, go to below

If the end buds are not noticeably larger than the side buds, go to next page

If the end buds are long (½–¾ inch), tapering very gradually on a stout twig, go to page 30

If the buds are less than ½ inch long, go to page 16

If the buds are almost an inch long, grow at a wide angle from the twig, and show eight or more scales, it is a BEECH. Go to below

If the buds lie close against the twig, and are about ½ inch long, showing five to six scales, it is **COMMON SERVICEBERRY or JUNEBERRY**
Amelanchier arborea
Usually a small tree, often shrublike, with bark gray with darker long streaks.

If the bark is a light, satiny gray, and it is a native tree of rich forests, it is **AMERICAN BEECH**
Fagus grandifolia

If the bark is a darker, pewter gray, and it is a planted tree on a lawn, it is **EUROPEAN BEECH**
Fagus sylvatica

illustration on next page →

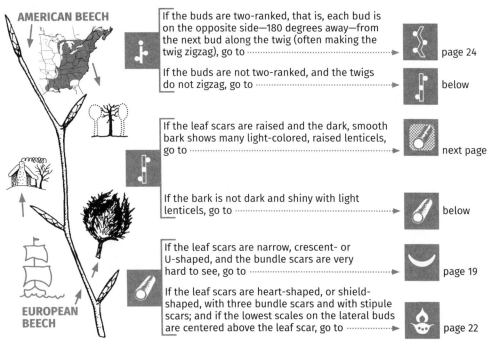

AMERICAN BEECH

If the buds are two-ranked, that is, each bud is on the opposite side—180 degrees away—from the next bud along the twig (often making the twig zigzag), go to ·········→ page 24

If the buds are not two-ranked, and the twigs do not zigzag, go to ·········→ below

If the leaf scars are raised and the dark, smooth bark shows many light-colored, raised lenticels, go to ·········→ next page

If the bark is not dark and shiny with light lenticels, go to ·········→ below

If the leaf scars are narrow, crescent- or U-shaped, and the bundle scars are very hard to see, go to ·········→ page 19

If the leaf scars are heart-shaped, or shield-shaped, with three bundle scars and with stipule scars; and if the lowest scales on the lateral buds are centered above the leaf scar, go to ·········→ page 22

EUROPEAN BEECH

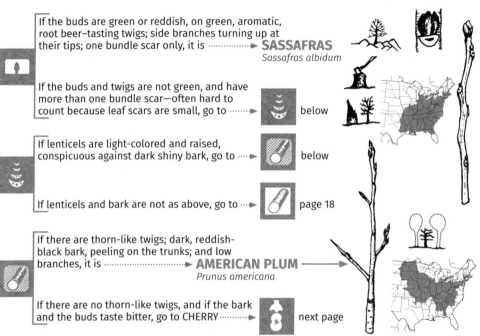

If the buds are green or reddish, on green, aromatic, root beer–tasting twigs; side branches turning up at their tips; one bundle scar only, it is ············▶ **SASSAFRAS**
Sassafras albidum

If the buds and twigs are not green, and have more than one bundle scar—often hard to count because leaf scars are small, go to ·······▶ below

If lenticels are light-colored and raised, conspicuous against dark shiny bark, go to ····▶ below

If lenticels and bark are not as above, go to ···▶ page 18

If there are thorn-like twigs; dark, reddish-black bark, peeling on the trunks; and low branches, it is ······················▶ **AMERICAN PLUM** ⟶
Prunus americana

If there are no thorn-like twigs, and if the bark and the buds taste bitter, go to CHERRY ·······▶ next page

17

If the buds have gray-margined scales, the lenticels do not elongate horizontally, and it is a small tree, it is ⋯⋯⋯⋯⋯▸ **CHOKECHERRY**
Prunus virginiana ⟶

If the bud scales are not gray-margined, and the lenticels do elongate horizontally, go to 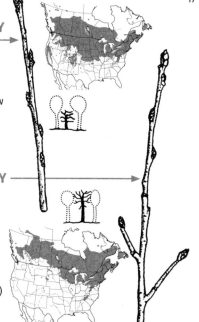 below

If the bark is dark, peeling in roundish flakes on older trunks; and it is a big tree, it is ⋯⋯▸ **BLACK CHERRY** ⟶
Prunus serotina

If the bark is lustrous orange red, with the lenticels orange and conspicuous and powdery on the surface, and if a few buds are clustered at the tip of the twig, it is ⋯⋯⋯⋯⋯⋯▸ **PIN CHERRY**
Prunus pensylvanica
(illustration on p. 10)

If the leaf scar is broadly crescent-shaped or triangular, showing three bundle scars or three groups of bundle scars, go to ⟶ below

If the leaf scar is very narrow, and bundle scars are very hard to see; and many-scarred fruiting spurs, or thorn-like twigs, often present, go to ⟶ next page

If the leaf scar is brown with lighter bundle scars; and buds are dark with downy tips with end bud only slightly larger than side buds, it is ⟶ **SOUR GUM or TUPELO** *Nyssa sylvatica*

Lower branches are usually declined. Mature trunks have "alligator bark."

If the leaf scars are not as above. and the pith is five-sided, go to ⟶ below

If bundle scars are white rings with dark center; twigs shiny, aromatic; branchlets developing corky ridges; trunk sometimes exuding an aromatic gum; and woody, ball-like fruits hanging on through the winter, it is ⟶ **SWEET GUM** *Liquidambar styraciflua*

If the lowest scale on a side bud is centered directly above the leaf scar; and a minute stipule scar may be seen at each side of the leaf scar, go to ⟶ page 22

If the buds are smooth, hairless, go to ··········→ page 21

If the buds and/or twigs are hairy, or have hairy tips, go to ···→ below

If the buds are blunt, and the tree large and broad, it is ·········→ **EUROPEAN WILD APPLE** *Malus sylvestris*

If some twigs have thorns (like stunted twigs); or if the buds have reddish outer scales, with a little of the woolly gray inner scales showing at the tip, it is a CRABAPPLE. Go to ·······→ below

If the twigs are smooth, it is ·······→ **SWEET CRABAPPLE** *Malus coronaria*

If the twigs are woolly, it is ········→ **PRAIRIE CRABAPPLE** *Malus ioensis*

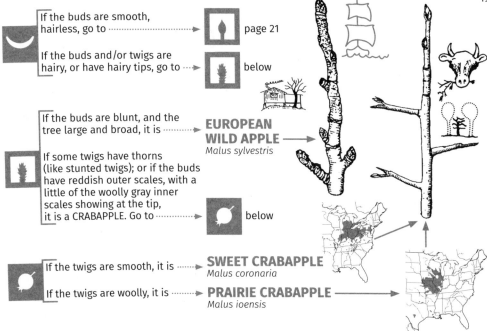

If the thorns are short (less than ¾ inch), and regularly spaced along the twig, go to ⟶ below

If there are thorns over ¾ inch long, and they are irregularly spaced, go to below

If the thorns are paired, it is **BLACK LOCUST**
Robinia pseudoacacia

If the thorns are single, on a twig that zigzags from thorn to thorn, it is **OSAGE ORANGE**
Maclura pomifera

Some old Osage Orange trees also have warty growths on the twigs.

If some of the thorns are branched, and no winter buds show, it is **HONEY LOCUST**
Gleditsia triacanthos
(illustration on p. 34)

If the thorns are not branched, and the winter buds show, it is **HAWTHORN**
(illustration on next page)

If the buds are smooth, pointed; and side buds are pointed away from the twig, it is **COMMON PEAR**
Pyrus communis →

If the buds are globular, and red, it is **HAWTHORN** →

Usually, this tree bears sharp, smooth thorns.

Hawthorns are far too numerous to cover here. You will probably be seeing one of these more common forms:

DOWNY HAWTHORN
Crataegus mollis

FROSTED HAWTHORN →
Crataegus pruinosa

COCKSPUR HAWTHORN
Crataegus crus-galli

WASHINGTON HAWTHORN →
Crataegus phaenopyrum

DOTTED HAWTHORN
Crataegus punctata

If the buds and twigs have a dense, white, cottony covering, easily rubbed off; and the tree has smooth, whitish bark with black markings, it is ·········→ **WHITE POPLAR**
Populus alba

There is a narrow form with ascending branches called Bolleana Poplar.

If the tree has no such dense white covering, and it is either spire-shaped or small, go to ·········→ below

If the tree is spire-shaped, with many ascending small branches, it is **LOMBARDY POPLAR**
Populus nigra

If the trees are small (with light-gray bark, darker at the base), often forming colonies, go to ·········→ next page

If the buds are shiny, pressed against the twig, it is ········· → **QUAKING ASPEN**
Populus tremuloides

If the buds are dusty gray and divergent, it is **BIGTOOTH ASPEN**
Populus grandidentata

If the tree has warty bark, becoming warty-ridged on the trunk, with very slender, zigzag twigs, it is ·············· **HACKBERRY**
Celtis occidentalis

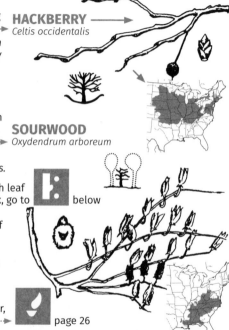

> *Dark, cherry-like fruit sometimes hangs on into the winter. The tree is often marked by clustered twigs called witches' brooms.*

If the bark is not warty, go to below

If the buds are very small, partially sunken in the bark of the twigs; and the leaf scar has a single bundle scar, it is ·············· **SOURWOOD**
Oxydendrum arboreum

> *Often shrublike, but tall in the mountains. Look for loose clusters of dry seed capsules.*

If there is more than one bundle scar on each leaf scar, and the buds are not hidden in the bark, go to below

If the buds are roughly centered over the leaf scar like this:

 go to next page

If the buds are *not* centered over the leaf scar, but are to one side, it is an ELM. Go to ·············· page 26

If the side buds are about the same width as the twig, the twigs light brown, go to ⟶  below

A full-sized tree with milky juice in spring.

If the side buds are wider than the twig; the leaf scars small, narrow, with unequal stipule scars, go to ⟶ below

A small tree without milky juice in spring.

If the twigs are downy, and if the buds are longer than wide with brown-margined bud scales, and spread away from the twig, it is **RED MULBERRY** ⟶

Morus rubra

If the twigs are not downy; and if the buds are pressed against the twig, almost as wide as long, often with additional small buds on either side it is ⟶ **WHITE MULBERRY**

Morus alba ⟶

If there are about six scales on each bud; and if the bark peels vertically in ½-inch strips, it is **IRONWOOD** (illustration on p. 39)

If the trunk is like gray stone sculpted into muscles and sinews, with about 12 scales on each bud, it is ⟶ **BLUE BEECH AMERICAN HORNBEAM**

Carpinus caroliniana ⟶

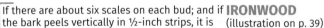

If the older twigs are corky-winged, or have corky growths, it is **CORK ELM** ────▶
Ulmus thomasii

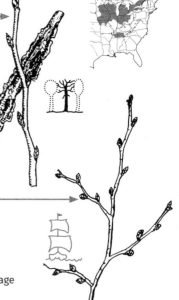

If the twigs are not corky, go to below

 If the twigs are very slender, holding many globular flower buds in addition to the other buds, it is **SIBERIAN ELM** ────▶
Ulmus pumila

If the twigs are not markedly slender, go to next page

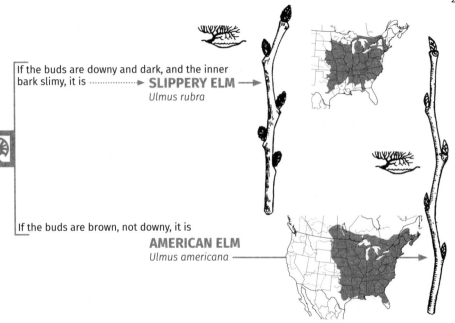

If the buds are downy and dark, and the inner bark slimy, it is ·················▶ **SLIPPERY ELM**
Ulmus rubra

If the buds are brown, not downy, it is
AMERICAN ELM
Ulmus americana

If the bud has hairy inner scales showing between two smooth outer scales, go to page 30

If the bud doesn't have hairy inner scales, go to below

If the scales meet as do the two parts of a duck bill and are smooth reddish brown; and the bud is stalked; and the pith triangular, it is **EUROPEAN ALDER**
Alnus glutinosa

If the two scales are overlapping, go to below

If the leaf scar has only one curved bundle scar (shriveled fruit may persist into the winter), it is **COMMON PERSIMMON**
Diospyros virginiana

If the leaf scar has three or more bundle scars, go to next page

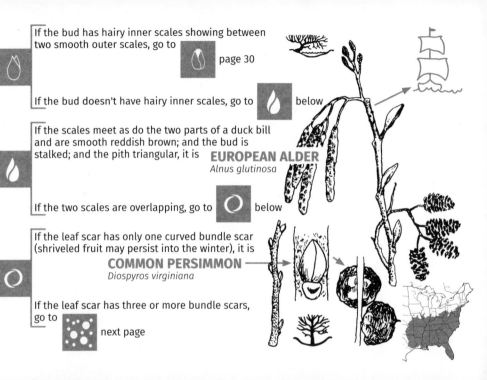

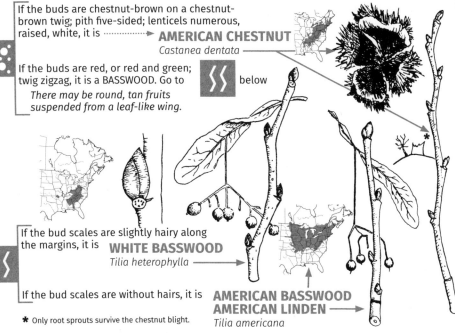

If the buds are chestnut-brown on a chestnut-brown twig; pith five-sided; lenticels numerous, raised, white, it is ·········▶ **AMERICAN CHESTNUT**
Castanea dentata

If the buds are red, or red and green; twig zigzag, it is a BASSWOOD. Go to below
There may be round, tan fruits suspended from a leaf-like wing.

If the bud scales are slightly hairy along the margins, it is **WHITE BASSWOOD**
Tilia heterophylla

If the bud scales are without hairs, it is **AMERICAN BASSWOOD AMERICAN LINDEN**
Tilia americana

✱ Only root sprouts survive the chestnut blight.

If the end bud is hairy and has its tip turned slightly to one side; the bark is marked with conspicuous light-colored lenticels; and the leaf scars are narrow, raised, it is a MOUNTAIN-ASH. Go to ············→ below

If the end bud is symmetrical; leaf scar crescent-shaped, with three bundle scars (or three groups of bundle scars); and the small branches are light-colored, smooth; the pith five-sided; and a small stipule scar may be seen on each side of the leaf scar; and the lowest scale on a side bud is centered and directly above the leaf scar, go to ········→ below

If the buds and twigs are woolly, it is **EUROPEAN MOUNTAIN-ASH**
Sorbus aucuparia

If the twigs are smooth, and the outer bud scales are sticky; but the inner scales, protruding at the tip, are hairy, and the tree is rather shrublike, it is **AMERICAN MOUNTAIN-ASH**
Sorbus americana

If the end buds are very long (often an inch or more), excessively resinous, fragrant; twigs reddish brown, it is either: ···············→ **BALSAM POPLAR**
Populus balsamifera
or: **BALM OF GILEAD**
Populus x jackii

(a cultivated tree usually grown from cuttings or sprouts of male plants and produces no seeds)

If the end buds are only about ½ inch long, go to next page

If the buds taper to both ends; twigs yellow to yellow brown, go to  below

If the buds are broadly egg-shaped; twigs brownish gray, it is **SWAMP COTTONWOOD**
Populus heterophylla

If the buds are sticky, it is
EASTERN COTTONWOOD
Populus deltoides

If the buds are slightly hairy, it is
PLAINS COTTONWOOD
Populus deltoides var. *monilifera*

If the twigs are long, pendulous, and slender; and the twigs and branchlets are yellow to orange, it is **WEEPING WILLOW** →
Salix babylonica

If the twigs and branchlets are not pendulous, go to below

If the twigs are yellowish, bark gray to brown, and twigs not brittle at their bases, go to next page

If the twigs and trunks are brown to almost black; and twigs have brittle bases that cause them to break off easily, it is **BLACK WILLOW**
Salix nigra →

If the twigs are greenish to yellow, with fine silky hairs, it is
WHITE WILLOW
Salix alba

One of the varieties of white willow, selected for its especially golden color, is known as golden willow.

If twigs are yellow to yellow brown, with large buds; leaf-scars U-shaped, it is
PEACHLEAF WILLOW
Salix amygdaloides

34

If the twigs are a lustrous red brown, and if they zigzag from leaf scar to leaf scar; and the tree has light-colored, horizontal lenticels on smooth bark, it is ·································➤ **HONEY LOCUST**
Gleditsia triacanthos

Mature trees usually have a spreading, dished top; bear long, branched thorns; and have flat, curved or twisted pods 6–8 inches long. A thornless, podless horticultural variety is commonly planted along streets and in parks.

If the twigs are not as above, go to below

If the twigs are not as above; or if there are pods 4 inches or less long, go to 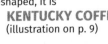 next page

If the twigs are thick, with thick, salmon-colored pith; two side buds, one above the other, can be seen above each leaf scar, appearing sunken and crater-shaped, it is
KENTUCKY COFFEETREE
(illustration on p. 9)

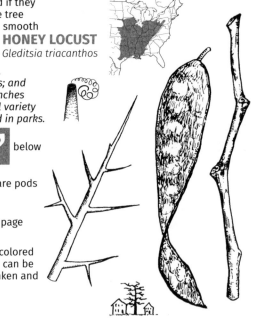

If the tree has an extremely broad and flat top; or if there are pods with the lower tip extremely long-tapered, it is

MIMOSA SILK TREE
Albizia julibrissin

If the top is not extremely broad and flat, go to

 below

If each winter bud is almost completely encircled by a leaf scar, it is

YELLOWWOOD
Cladrastis kentukea

If the winter bud is not encircled; and if there are globular flower buds appearing in many places along the bark—even sometimes on the trunk—it is

REDBUD
Cercis canadensis

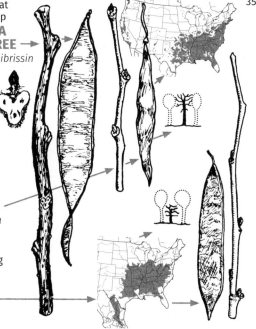

If the buds are pale and downy; the pith is in thin, horizontal layers; and the lenticels are round; and the vein scars form three crescents on the leaf scar, it is a WALNUT. Go to page 38

Any nuts you find under the tree will have husks that do not split open, but they will stain your fingers brown.

If the pith is not layered, but is somewhat five-sided, and the lenticels are elongated, it is a HICKORY. Go to below

If the terminal bud is mustard yellow, flattened, granular, and the tree is usually on bottomland, it is ⟶ **BITTERNUT HICKORY** ⟶

Carya cordiformis

The husk is yellowish, thin-skinned, four-ribbed above the middle. The nut is globe-shaped, thin-shelled. The kernel is bitter.

If the buds are not yellow and flattened, go to  below

If the terminal bud is large (½ inch or more), with dark outer scales; and if the bark peels in great thick plates, giving the tree a shaggy appearance, it is

SHAGBARK HICKORY
Carya ovata

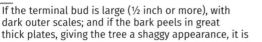

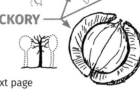

The husk of the nut is dark brown; the nut is four-ribbed, thick-walled.

If the terminal bud is not large and dark, go to next page

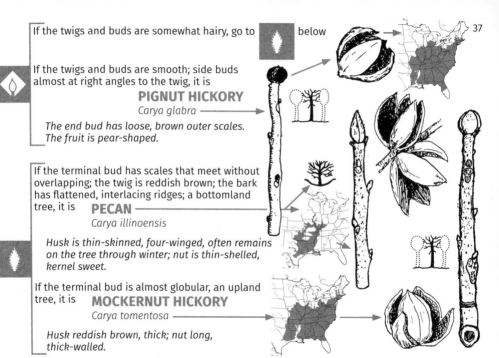

If the twigs and buds are somewhat hairy, go to the image below

If the twigs and buds are smooth; side buds almost at right angles to the twig, it is
PIGNUT HICKORY
Carya glabra

The end bud has loose, brown outer scales. The fruit is pear-shaped.

If the terminal bud has scales that meet without overlapping; the twig is reddish brown; the bark has flattened, interlacing ridges; a bottomland tree, it is **PECAN**
Carya illinoensis

Husk is thin-skinned, four-winged, often remains on the tree through winter; nut is thin-shelled, kernel sweet.

If the terminal bud is almost globular, an upland tree, it is **MOCKERNUT HICKORY**
Carya tomentosa

Husk reddish brown, thick; nut long, thick-walled.

38

If the end bud is cream-colored and one to two times as long as it is wide; and the leaf scars have a velvety strip across the top; and the pith is dark brown, with layers as thick as the spaces between the layers; and if the bark has light-colored, flattened ridges making a network against the darker brown, it is ·········▶ **BUTTERNUT** ──────▶
WHITE WALNUT
Juglans cinerea

The fruit is oblong.

If the end bud is gray, short; the side buds are set in a notch in the upper edge of the leaf scar; the pith is light brown, with layers much smaller than the spaces between the layers; and the bark is dark and furrowed, it is **BLACK WALNUT** ──────▶
Juglans nigra

The fruit is globular.

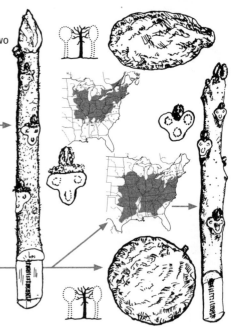

If the bark is thin, and glove-smooth, or peeling, or if it is ragged, it is a BIRCH. Go to ·······▶ below

If the bark is not thin, go to below

 If the trunks are white with some black markings, go to next page

If the trunks are yellowish to red brown, go to page 41

 If the trunk has long, square-ended strips of bark peeling upward; and the twigs are slender, it is **IRONWOOD**
Ostrya virginiana

If there are cones (stiff ones not breaking apart between your fingers or in the wind) as well as catkins; the buds are smooth and stalked; and the pith triangular, it is **EUROPEAN ALDER**
Alnus glutinosa
(illustration on p. 28)

If the catkins are usually borne singly at the tips of the twigs; and the bark cannot be easily split into thin layers and is marked with black triangles, it is ········→ **GRAY BIRCH** ————————→
Betula populifolia

If the bark peels into thin layers, go to 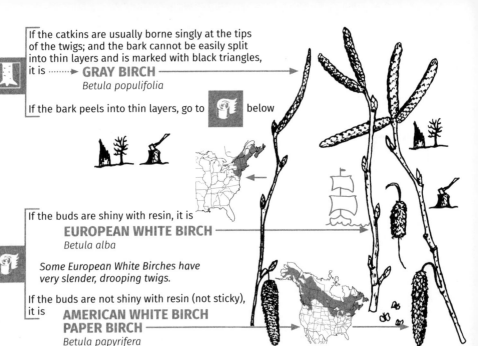 below

If the buds are shiny with resin, it is
EUROPEAN WHITE BIRCH ————————→
Betula alba

Some European White Birches have very slender, drooping twigs.

If the buds are not shiny with resin (not sticky), it is
AMERICAN WHITE BIRCH
PAPER BIRCH ————————→
Betula papyrifera

If the bark is peeling, and silvery yellow to copper red, go to below.

If the bark is dark brown, not peeling, and the tree resembles a cherry tree (the twigs and buds are good to chew for a strong wintergreen taste; the cones are upright and thick and persist into the winter) it is **CHERRY BIRCH**
Betula lenta

If the tree trunk is excessively ragged; and the twigs are hairy, it is **BLACK BIRCH RIVER BIRCH**
Betula nigra

The cones have matured and fallen apart during the summer.

If the bark is silvery to pale yellow, somewhat ragged, and the twigs have a slight wintergreen flavor, it is ·········▶ **YELLOW BIRCH**
Betula alleghaniensis

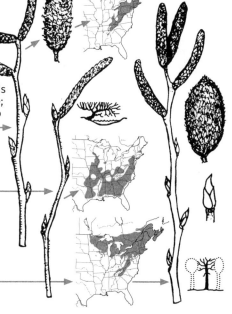

42

 If the end bud is hairy or woolly, go to next page

If the end bud is smooth, go to below

 If the end bud is 1½–2 inches long; the bark thin, dark brown, it is ·············▶ **MOUNTAIN MAGNOLIA**
Magnolia fraseri

If the end bud is 1 inch long, with its tip pointed and curved; the bark thick, gray; and the tree often branching at the base, it is **UMBRELLA MAGNOLIA** ⟶
Magnolia tripetala

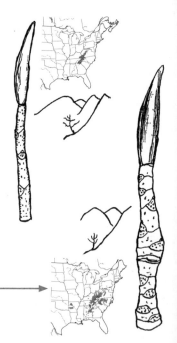

If the hairy covering is silky, go to below

If the hairy covering is woolly, matted; the buds are 1¾–2 inches long; and the new growth light yellow-green, it is

BIGLEAF MAGNOLIA
Magnolia macrophylla ⟶

If the end bud is oblong, ½–¾ inch long; densely covered with olive-gray hairs; the new growth a shining reddish brown; the bark dark gray brown, furrowed; and the tree pyramidal, it is

CUCUMBER MAGNOLIA
Magnolia acuminata ⟶

If the end bud is egg-shaped, silky, gray; the new growth reddish brown, the bark gray, smooth, it is

SAUCER MAGNOLIA
Magnolia x soulangeana ⟶

× ⅓

If the entire twig is ¼ inch or more thick, and the terminal bud is oval and conspicuous, go to next page

If the entire twig is not ¼ inch or more thick, or does not have an oval, conspicuous end bud, go to below

If the terminal buds are rough and dry; and the bundle scars form an almost continuous line on the shield-shaped or oval leaf scar, it is an ASH. Go to page 46

The seed is at the end of a symmetrical, flat wing.

If the terminal buds are not rough and dry; and the leaf scars are narrow, inconspicuous, with three bundle scars, go to below

If you find winged seeds, they will not be symmetrical.

If there is a notched line encircling the twig, connecting each pair of leaf scars; and if the tree has two kinds of buds: conspicuous, onion-shaped buds; and inconspicuous, or concealed buds, it is

FLOWERING DOGWOOD
Cornus florida

A small tree with alligator bark when mature. There may be red fruits still on the tree.

If the leaf scars are somewhat V-shaped, with three bundle scars; and the end bud is egg-shaped or cone-shaped, it is a MAPLE. Go to page 48

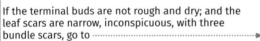

If the terminal bud is sticky, dark, smooth, and ¾ inch or more long, it is
HORSE CHESTNUT
Aesculus hippocastanum ⟶

If the terminal bud is not as above, go to below

If the bud scales are keeled, like a boat bottom, and have fine-hairy edges; and if the twigs, when bruised, have a fetid odor, it is
OHIO BUCKEYE
Aesculus glabra

In fall, look on the ground for the spiny husks holding single seeds with large, pale scars.

If the bud scales are not keeled, it is
SWEET BUCKEYE
YELLOW BUCKEYE
Aesculus flava

In fall, look on the ground for leathery husks that usually hold two smooth seeds.

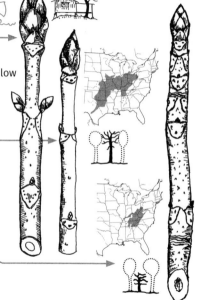

If the twigs are four-sided; the bark breaking into plates; the seed occupying half the length of the wide wing, it is **BLUE ASH**
Fraxinus quadrangulata

If the twigs are not four-sided, go to below

If the leaf scar is notched at the top so that it is somewhat horseshoe shaped; the wing portion of the fruit is narrow, about 3/16 inch wide; and the bark is ridged, forming diamond-shaped areas, it is ·········· **WHITE ASH**
Fraxinus americana

If the leaf scar is semicircular or oval, go to next page

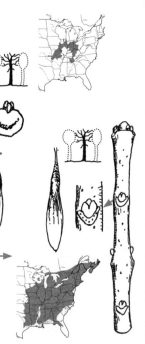

If the buds and new twigs are rusty-hairy; and the inner face of the outer bark is reddish, it is ··········► **RED ASH**
Fraxinus pennsylvanica

If the buds and new twigs are not rusty-hairy, go to below

If the buds are very dark (nearly black); and the trunk bark is smooth, soft-scaly, easily rubbed off, it is ·······► **BLACK ASH**
Fraxinus nigra

Seed wings are broad, blunt, and notched.

If the buds are red brown, and the trunk bark is ridged, and firmer, it is a variety of Red Ash called ··························► **GREEN ASH**
Fraxinus pennsylvanica var. subintegerrima

Seed wings are narrow, tapered, not notched.

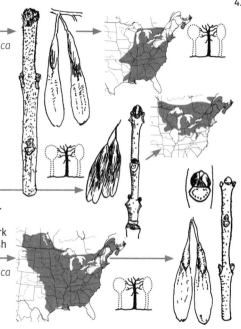

If the buds are red; and the new growth on the twigs is red or red brown, go to below

If the buds and the new growth are not red, go to next page

If the tree is shrublike, an understory tree of the forest, with densely hairy twigs (often with fruits that hang on into the winter), it is ·····▶ **MOUNTAIN MAPLE** ───▶

Acer spicatum

If the tree is not shrublike, and the flower buds are globular and conspicuous, go to below

If the twigs give a rank smell when broken, the bark on old trunks peels in great shaggy flakes, and the bud scales are pointed, it is **SILVER MAPLE**

Acer saccharinum

If the younger trunks are smooth, very pale gray, with darker markings, and if the twigs do not have a rank smell when broken, and if the bud scales are rounded, it is ···············▶ **RED MAPLE** ───▶

Acer rubrum

If the buds are whitish and woolly; the twigs are purplish or greenish; and the leaf scars from opposite sides of the twig meet at their tips, forming a tooth-like point, it is **BOX ELDER**
Acer negundo

If the buds are not whitish and woolly, go below to

If the twigs are stout, with end buds making a broad, low triangle, smooth, green or partly green, go to below

If the buds are longer-pointed, and brown to reddish brown, go to next page

If the buds are marked with green and some reddish brown; and the fruits, which may still be clinging to the tree, are joined in pairs at a wide angle so that they resemble a miniature coat hanger, it is **NORWAY MAPLE**
Acer platanoides

In early spring, the tree is conspicuous with clusters of yellow-green flowers. At that time one can easily identify this tree by its milky juice.

If the end buds are big and green, it is **SYCAMORE MAPLE**
No milky juice.   *Acer pseudoplatanus*

If the tree is small, shrublike (usually on sandy soil); the bark is striped with light lines; the buds have short stalks; the end bud has two scales that meet at their edges but do not overlap; and the bud scales are keeled, it is **STRIPED MAPLE** →
Acer pensylvanicum

If the tree is not shrublike; if the buds are brown to grayish brown; the twigs slender; and the bark stone-gray with large scales peeling off sideways on the old trunks (usually marked by horizontal rows of yellow-bellied sapsuckers' holes), it is ········► **SUGAR MAPLE** ——►
Acer saccharum

If the twigs are rough-hairy; and the buds are dark gray to black; and the bark is very dark, almost black, it may be a tree similar to sugar maple called ········► **BLACK MAPLE**
Acer nigrum

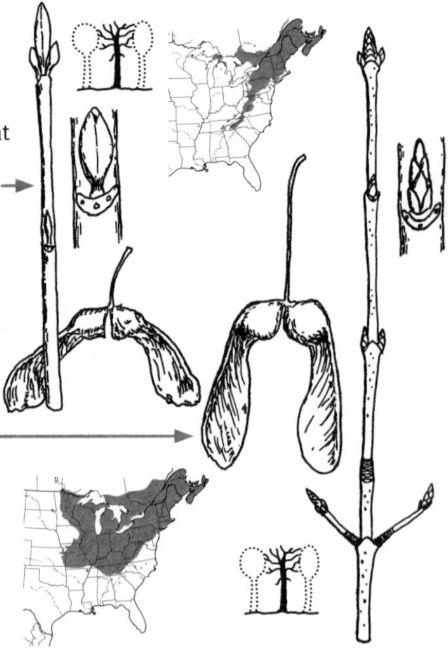

If the bark is light gray on younger parts, flaky or ridged and darker gray on older parts; and if the buds are only about ⅛–¼ inch long, go to below

Leaves you may find will not be bristle-tipped. The acorn ripens in one year. The inside of the acorn cup is smooth.

If the bark is dark, smooth and shiny on the younger parts, becoming ridged on the older parts; and if the buds are conical or ovate, ⅛ to ½ inch long, go to page 54

The leaves will usually be bristle-tipped. The acorns, which are bitter, take two years to ripen. So you may find both young ones on the branches and ripe ones on the ground. The acorn cup is silky or woolly inside and has thin scales.

 If the buds are rounded, go to next page

If the buds are pointed, go to below

 If the buds are chestnut brown with hairless scales; the bark flaky; the crown narrow, and dense; and the tree has a buttressed base (often grows on limestone ridges), it is **CHINQUAPIN OAK** *Quercus muehlenbergii*

If the buds are dark red with hairy scales; the bark is deeply fissured, not flaky; the inner bark is red; and the tree has an open, spreading crown, it is **CHESTNUT OAK** *Quercus michauxii*

If you can easily rub off a handful of bark scales from the trunk, go below ·····

If the trunk bark is furrowed, but has few scales to rub off, go to next page ·····

If the twigs are smooth, and the tree has a broad, rugged crown, go below ·····

If the young twigs are covered with coarse, orange-brown down; and the tree is often scrubby and irregular and usually on dry, sandy, or rocky upland, it is ·····► **POST OAK**
Quercus stellata

Look for durable, leathery leaves, lobed to form a sort of cross-shape. Acorn cup bowl-shaped, and half encloses the nut.

If the acorns are long and paired on long stalks; and the tree is planted in a park or parkway, it is

If the acorns are not stalked, and the tree is a native, it is ·····► **WHITE OAK**

ENGLISH OAK
Quercus robur

Quercus alba

Look for right-angled branching. The pale-tan leaves cling far into winter. The acorns will be hard to find because they are sweet squirrel food. White oaks are often unmistakably marked by a belt of worn-looking bark on the trunk (caused by fungus).

If the twigs are thick and somewhat hairy, developing corky ridges with age; and the buds are hairy, it is **BUR OAK** ——————

Quercus macrocarpa

The end buds often show thread-like stipules longer than the scales. Look for acorns almost covered by the fringed acorn cups. This is the most gnarled and rugged-looking of the oaks.

If the twigs are smooth, the lower branches hang down, and the tree grows in rather moist soil, and there are often curling scales of bark on the branches, it is

SWAMP WHITE OAK ——————

Quercus bicolor

Look for acorns with stems 1–4 inches long.

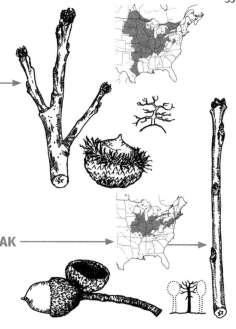

If the tree is small (never over 30 feet), with a crooked trunk and contorted branches; or if it is shrubby, go to next page

These trees usually grow on barren, dry ridges.

If the tree is of normal shape and size, and not contorted or shrubby, go below

These trees usually grow in a forest or in open groves on good upland or bottomland soil.

If the tree is branched like a pine tree, with a straight central trunk going almost to the very top, and with drooping lower branches, it is **PIN OAK**
Quercus palustris

Straight-up-growth habit makes this a common tree for planting along roads near powerlines.

If the tree is not branched like a pine tree, go to below

If the bud scales are covered with a grayish wool; the buds decidedly angular, up to ½ inch long; and the inner bark is yellow, it is **BLACK OAK**
Quercus velutina

The most reliable way to identify black oak is by a fringe around the edge of the acorn cup, formed by the loose tips of the scales.

If the bud scales are not covered with a grayish wool (though there may be some hairiness); if the buds are not noticeably angular; and the inner bark is not yellow, go to next page

Acorn cup scales are not loose and form no fringe.

If the buds are all less than ⅛ inch long, it is
SCRUB OAK →
BEAR OAK
Quercus ilicifolia
This tree is shrubby, with abundant small acorns less than ½ inch long.

If the buds are more than ⅛ inch long, it is **BLACKJACK OAK** →
The acorns are about ¾ inch long, light brown, and striated.
Quercus marilandica

If the lower part of the tree is conspicuously cluttered with dead branches and twigs, it is ·······················→ **HILL'S OAK** —
NORTHERN PIN OAK
Quercus ellipsoidalis
The acorn cup is top-shaped.

If the tree is not conspicuously cluttered, the tree is either Scarlet Oak, Shingle Oak, Water Oak, Red Oak, Spanish Oak, or Willow Oak. To find out which, it is necessary to look at an acorn (or a dry leaf). Go to ··→ next page

If the acorn cup is top-shaped, like this: go to below

If the acorn cup is more saucer-shaped, like this: go to next page

If the acorns are on short stalks; and the tree has gray-brown, shallowly furrowed bark; green-brown twigs; and brown leaves persisting until spring, it is

x ⅓

SHINGLE OAK
Quercus imbricaria

If there are concentric rings around the tip of the acorn; and if the tree has blackish, deeply furrowed bark and red-brown twigs, it is

Look for red inner bark.

SCARLET OAK
Quercus coccinea

x ⅙

If the acorns are nearly black, with a bright-orange kernel, it is ··········► **WATER OAK**
Quercus nigra

Leathery leaves of several forms cling on this tree far into the winter.

   x ⅙

If the acorns and kernels are not as above, go to below

If the acorns are ½–1 inch long; and the scales on the acorn cup are without hair; and there are long smooth surfaces on the ridge of the bark, it is ··················► **NORTHERN RED OAK**
Quercus rubra ─────────►

This is the most often-planted American Oak in Europe.

 x 1/16

If the acorns are ½ inch or less long, and the scales on the acorn cup are hairy, go to ··········► next page

58

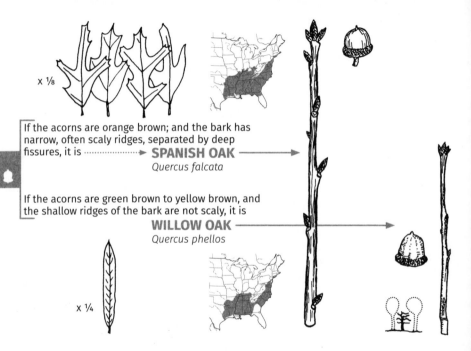

x ⅛

If the acorns are orange brown; and the bark has narrow, often scaly ridges, separated by deep fissures, it is ·················· ► **SPANISH OAK** ——
Quercus falcata

If the acorns are green brown to yellow brown, and the shallow ridges of the bark are not scaly, it is

WILLOW OAK ——
Quercus phellos

x ¼

INDEX

Other books in the pocket-size *Finder* series:

FOR US AND CANADA EAST OF THE ROCKIES

Berry Finder native plants with fleshy fruits
Bird Finder frequently seen birds
Bird Nest Finder aboveground nests
Fern Finder native ferns of the Midwest and Northeast
Flower Finder spring wildflowers and flower families
Life on Intertidal Rocks organisms of the North Atlantic Coast
Scat Finder mammal scat
Track Finder mammal tracks and footprints
Tree Finder native and common introduced trees
Winter Weed Finder dry plants in winter

FOR THE PACIFIC COAST

Pacific Coast Bird Finder frequently seen birds
Pacific Coast Fish Finder marine fish of the Pacific Coast
Pacific Coast Mammal Finder mammals, their tracks, skulls, and other signs
Pacific Coast Tree Finder native trees, from Sitka to San Diego

FOR THE PACIFIC COAST *(continued)*

Pacific Intertidal Life organisms of the Pacific Coast
Redwood Region Flower Finder wildflowers of the coastal fog belt of CA

FOR ROCKY MOUNTAIN AND DESERT STATES

Desert Tree Finder desert trees of CA, AZ, NM
Rocky Mountain Flower Finder wildflowers below tree line
Rocky Mountain Mammal Finder mammals, their tracks, skulls, and other signs
Rocky Mountain Tree Finder native Rocky Mountain trees

FOR STARGAZERS

Constellation Finder patterns in the night sky and star stories

FOR FORAGERS

Mushroom Finder fungi of North America

NATURE STUDY GUIDES are published by AdventureKEEN, 2204 1st Ave. S., Suite 102, Birmingham, AL 35233; 800-678-7006; naturestudy.com. See shop.adventurewithkeen.com for our full line of nature and outdoor activity guides by ADVENTURE PUBLICATIONS, MENASHA RIDGE PRESS, and WILDERNESS PRESS, including many guides for birding, wildflowers, rocks, and trees, plus regional and national parks, hiking, camping, backpacking, and more.